Kenelm Digby Beste

A May chaplet and other verses for the month of Mary

Kenelm Digby Beste

A May chaplet and other verses for the month of Mary

ISBN/EAN: 9783742860279

Manufactured in Europe, USA, Canada, Australia, Japa

Cover: Foto ©Lupo / pixelio.de

Manufactured and distributed by brebook publishing software (www.brebook.com)

Kenelm Digby Beste

A May chaplet and other verses for the month of Mary

A MAY CHAPLET,

And other Verses

FOR THE MONTH OF MARY.

Translated and Original.

BY

KENELM DIGBY BESTE,
Priest of the Oratory of S. Philip Neri.

London:
R. WASHBOURNE, 18 PATERNOSTER ROW.
1873.

PREFACE.

THE May Chaplet consists of Thirty-one Hymns, translated from "Les Guirlandes de Mai" of FATHER PHILPIN DE RIVIÈRES, of our Congregation.

To these I have added, with his sanction, The Seven Dolours and other Poems of my own in honour of Our Blessed Lady, which may not be thought out of place in a book of Verses for the Month of Mary.

K. D. B.

The Oratory,
    London, 1873.

CONTENTS.

	Page.
PRELUDE ...	xiii

TRANSLATIONS.

Les Violettes; or, The May Chaplet—

	Page
CROWN HER WITH FAIR FLOWERS (Couronnons-la de fleurs)	1
1. MYSTICAL PEARL (Perle mystique)...	4
2. THE CRADLE OF MARY (Au berceau de Marie)...	8
3. AWAKE (Réveillez-vous ô sainte Enfant!)	11
4. HAD I BUT SEEN HER! (Ah! si je l'avais vue!)...	14
5. HER HYMNS (Ses cantiques) ...	18
6. THE GOD OF MARY (Dieu de Marie) ...	21
7. MARY A REVELATION OF GOD (Dieu révélé dans Marie)	25
8. THE AVOWAL OF S. BERNARDINE OF SIENA (Déclaration de saint Bernardin de Sienne) ...	28
9. AVE MARIA (L'Ave Maria) ...	30

CONTENTS.

	Page
10. CHRISTMAS AND COMMUNION (Noël et Communion) ...	33
11. THE HEAVENLY SAMARITAN (La Céleste Samaritaine)...	35
12. THE DREAM OF S. KATHERINE (Le Songe de sainte Catherine)...	38
13. BENEDICTION AT NOTRE DAME DES VICTOIRES (La Bénédiction de Notre-Dame des Victoires)	41
14. THEY HAVE NO WINE (Ils n'ont pas de vin)...	44
15. THE BLESSED SACRAMENT (Le Très-Saint-Sacrement) ...	47
16. THE SEVEN DOLOURS (Les Sept douleurs)	51
17. WOMAN! BEHOLD THY SON (Femme, voilà votre Fils!)	56
18. THE BRIDE OF THE HOLY GHOST (A Marie, Épouse du saint Esprit)	60
19. BLESSEDNESS (Le Bonheur)	63
20. WHERE MUST WE SEEK OUR MOTHER (Où la chercer?)	65
21. VIRGO PRUDENTISSIMA	69
22. THE PROCESSION OF VIRGINS (La Procession virginale)	73
23. HYMN OF LOVE (Chant d'amour)	76
24. SHOW THY FACE (Soulevez votre voile)	80
25. REVELATRIX (Révélatrice)	83
26. THE VISION OF S. PHILIP (La Vision de saint Philippe de Néri)	86
27. OUR LADY OF THE MIRACULOUS MEDAL (La Vierge de la médaille miraculeuse)	89
28. SPEAK TO MY HEART (Parlez à mon cœur)...	93
29. THE SERVANT OF MARY (Son service)	96
30. INTERCEDE (Intercédez pour nous)...	100
31. VENI CORONABERIS	103

CONTENTS.

ORIGINAL POEMS.

The Seven Dolours.

	Page.
1. The Prophecy of Simeon	109
2. The Flight into Egypt	113
3. The Three Days' Loss	119
4. Meeting Jesus with the Cross	124
5. The Crucifixion	129
6. The Taking down from the Cross	133
7. The Burial of Jesus	138
Our Blessed Lady's Communion on Holy Thursday	142
Ave Maria	146
Innocence and Penance	173

MAY is the month of flowers :
    Bring them one by one,
Fresh with heaven's showers,
    Fit for Mary's Son.
Take, Queen of May ! the gifts we bring,
In crowning thee, we crown our King.

May is the month of flowers :
    For the Saviour's Head
Bring from fragrant bowers
    Roses white and red.
We pierced with thorns that Sacred Brow,
Ah ! let us offer garlands now.

May is the month of flowers:
    Mother ! bless this wreath—
Thoughts for tranquil hours,
    Prayers thy sons may breathe !
O gentlest King ! vouchsafe to take
These lowly flowers, for Mary's sake !

A MAY CHAPLET.

For the Eve.

CROWN HER WITH FAIR FLOWERS.

> *The flowers have appeared in our land, the time for pruning is come: the voice of the turtle is heard in our land.* CANT. ii. 12.

Now Spring returns, and gentle doves
   Coo softly in each wooded dale,
   The liquid-voicèd nightingale
Sings to the sleeping air-rocked groves—
     While Spring decks field and prairie,
       Spreads leaflets over bowers,
      Praise we most holy Mary,
       And crown her with fair flowers.

Children we are: our flowers must prove,
   Like the frail fancies of our mind,
   Too poor to be in wreaths entwined,
To crown the Mother of fair love.
      They strew the Sanctuary,
         Fast fading with the hours,
      Yet praise most holy Mary,
         And crown her with fair flowers.

Ah! Mary is herself our Spring—
   She comes, and wintry frosts depart—
   She breathes, and soon the icy heart
Melts into songs of sorrowing.
      Of love no more be chary,
         But sing with new-born powers;
      Praise, praise most holy Mary,
         And crown her with fair flowers.

Dark Winter to the north makes wing,
   The Lord is Mary's sun and light,
   And even here, for her delight,
Begins the everlasting Spring.

Sweet scents, that ever vary,
    Revive these souls of ours
To praise most holy Mary,
    And crown her with fair flowers.

At last set free, the captive heart
   Can love, adore, and bless Thee, Lord;
Thrilled like a living harpsichord,
It sings how dear and good Thou art.
    Breathe, soft winds of the prairie,
      Fall, fall, ye gentle showers,
    Whilst we praise holy Mary,
      And crown her with fair flowers.

To Mary we must consecrate
   The canticles of love's own choice,
   Glad victory shall lend her voice,
And cheer us on to Heaven's gate.
    In God's own Sanctuary,
      In Sion's golden towers,
    We'll praise most holy Mary,
      And crown her with fair flowers.

THE MAY CHAPLET.

I.

MYSTICAL PEARL.

> *The Kingdom of Heaven is like to a merchant seeking good pearls. Who, when he had found one pearl of great price, went his way, and sold all that he had, and bought it.* ST. MATT. xiii. 45-46.
>
> *This pearl is also the Blessed Virgin Mary.* CORNELIUS A LAPIDE.

HAIL ! precious Pearl of God,
  Of world-wide fame and worth,
Thy grace-begirt abode
  Felt no sin-wave of Earth ;
The storm sped on its road,
  But spared thy place of birth.

MYSTICAL PEARL.

What should my purpose be,
   Throughout life's pilgrimage,
Except to search for thee,
   Most noble heritage ?—
To win thee worthily,
   My all I would engage.

Where art thou to be sought—
   In heaven, or here below?
Should love's bright lamp be brought,
   And hearts to seek thee go—
Or will a prayerful thought
   Discern thy gentle glow ?

O, had I to resign
   A sceptre and a crown,
How soon, to call thee mine,
   Sweet Pearl ! I'd lay them down,
To see thee softly shine,
   To have thee for mine own !

Where, then, shall I prepare
    Thy chosen place of rest?
May heart like mine e'en dare
    To claim thee for its guest—
There laid, like snow-flake fair
    On some red rose's breast?

Upon my brow how clear
    The softness of thy light!
What music for mine ear!
    If there, throughout the night
Thou whisper: Love is near,
    Rest safely in His sight!

O, deem not me too bold,
    Be Love's betrothal ring!
My hand were blest to hold,
    Midst toil, so fair a thing,
Within its bed of gold
    For ever slumbering!

MYSTICAL PEARL.

Dear Talisman! through thee,
   Though armies stand arrayed,
I gain the victory,
   Secure celestial aid,
And claim His clemency,
   Who loves the Pearl He made.

THE MAY CHAPLET.

II.

THE CRADLE OF MARY.

> *Who is she that cometh forth as the morning rising?* CANT. vi. 9.

My soul, behold this wondrous sight—
  An angel multitude descends,
And, lustrous with refulgent light,
  O'er one sweet cradled Infant bends.

Here sleeps God's purest, chosen Pearl,
  Hid, as in alabaster cave,
Here beauties doth His Rose unfurl,
  Whilst round her sheltering lilies wave.

THE CRADLE OF MARY.

This cradle—'Tis morn's azure sky,
   Day-silvered with its tranquil Star
By Light divine, fast drawing nigh
   To shine on nations from afar.

Let all creation gladly pay
   Meet homage to the Morning Star,
That warns the gloomy night away,
   And guides the Sun's resplendent car.

White-shadowed, Jordan's spotless dove
   Doth o'er the crystal waters glide—
Descending on like wings of love,
   The Spirit hovers o'er His Bride.

The Father watches from on high,
   A daughter in this little child,
The Word, with filial piety,
   Reveres His Mother undefiled.

Your infants, Christian matrons, bring,
   'Midst Mary's angels let them play—
Come, Virgins, in life's opening spring,
   Let innocence its worship pay.

We sinners, too, will venture in—
   With heavy heart yet noiseless tread—
And silently bewail our sin,
   Around this spotless cradle-bed.

III.

AWAKE!

> *Arise, make haste, my love, my dove.* CANT. ii. 10.

The day is passed away, the stars of night
   Steal forth, their timid watch to keep,
The Maiden rests in God's protecting sight—
   O dearest Child, sleep, sweetly sleep!

A transport hushed her song; but o'er her soul
   Ecstatic waves of love still sweep,
And on her brow still rests love's aureole,—
   O gentlest Child, sleep, sweetly sleep!

Most tranquilly she breathes, her features wear
    The look of rest—yet Anne may creep,
And catch the music of a murmured prayer—
    O holy Child, sleep, sweetly sleep!

Her very dreams in science far excel
    The wisest cherub's knowledge deep;
Far, far above the power of man to tell—
    O purest Child, sleep, sweetly sleep!

Alas! my life is but a guilty dream,
    For which I ought to blush and weep—
Remorse hangs o'er me with its sword-like gleam—
    O sinless Child, no longer sleep!

O rescue me when wandering near the brink
    Of danger, and sin's fatal leap
Into the dark abyss where lost souls sink—
    O wisest Child, no longer sleep!

O pray that never sleep, of God unblest,
   The senses of my soul may steep—
But may my heart be watchful whilst I rest—
   O holy Child, no longer sleep!

One night must come—O Mother! then be near—
   When death shall bring his slumber deep,
Then whisper softly in my dying ear:
   "My own poor child, sleep, sweetly sleep!"

IV.

HAD I BUT SEEN HER!

> *I purposed, therefore, to take her to me to live with me: knowing that she will communicate to me of her good things, and will be a comfort in my cares and griefs.*
> WISDOM viii. 9.

WOULD that my lot had been to contemplate
   The dawn which banished darkness from the earth,
The Star, whose shining did illuminate
   God's highest angels with fresh joy and mirth.
     "O Child, the Rose of endless love—
        For ever lives,
        And blooms above,
     And to all ages fragrance gives."

Oh, could I but have seen that infancy—
  Those ecstasies her parents oft beheld!
O what a heaven! for them each day to see
  New grace and beauty, which fresh love compelled.
    "Oh, Child of Mary, Thou must not repine,
        Thy grief control!
        Her gifts are thine—
    Each day adorn with them thy soul."

O Sion's Temple! would that I had dwelt
  Within the precincts of thy sacred wall
When God's Ark came—the tender Child who felt,
  Though but three years, the Eternal's call!
    "Her Heart, Child, is God's Temple now,
        Where all find grace,
        And never vow
    Was uttered in a nobler place."

Oh, had my heart but been the harpsichord
  To which she sang with more than angel skill!
It would have broken at each thrilling word,
  Or, filled with melody, would vibrate still.

"Child, when thy soul on wing of dove
    To heaven has flown,
    She, Harp of love,
Will aid its Sanctus at the Throne."

Oh, had I only seen her in the cave,
    Been trusted with the Child—received one kiss—
Received but one of those sweet looks they gave,
    My heart and breast would burn with speechless bliss!
    "O Child, God is a God of fire!
        His Mother will
        To love's desire
    Accede,—and give thee Jesus still."

Had I but waited in the Upper Room
    With Mary, in the days of Pentecost—
Ah! there, at Mary's feet would be my home,
    The Tabernacle of the Holy Ghost.
    "The Bride of Christ has since become
        His Mother's care,
        Thy Mother's home,
    Child, thou art with her everywhere!"

But, to have missed her last words, and her smile !
  The day her soul departed to her Love ;
When death was sent to guard the couch awhile,
  Till That which slept was also called above !
    " Child, wait—a little longer wait !
      'Tis but a night—
      They'll pass thy gate,
    And take thee to the land of light."

V.

HER HYMNS.

> *Mary, the prophetess, took a timbrel in her hand, and all the women went forth after her with timbrels and with dances; and she began this song unto them, saying: Let us sing to the Lord, for he is gloriously magnified.*
> Ex. xv. 20.

AT eve the little Virgin's hand
   Awoke the music of her lyre,
Her song was heard in heaven's land,
   Her chanting hushed the angel choir.
The Temple's echoes hung around,
   And trembled like the spell-bound air,
Oh! voice had never sweeter sound,
   Heart never breathed a purer prayer.

Alas ! that matchless melody,
   Excelling heaven's sweetest strain—
Those hymns of plaintive prophecy
   Will never more be heard again ;
What echo could repeat her songs ?
   What virgin saint could sing her hymn,
What angel of those countless throngs,
   What Sanctus-chanting seraphim ?

On earth the memory alone
   Remains to us of her sweet notes—
Just as around an altar-throne
   The fragrant scent of incense floats—
The slender column lightly rose,
   And vanished in the lofty dome,
The perfume lingers, and it shows
   Our Saviour's sacramental home.

What happiness ! O Virgin blest,
   To hear the music of thy hymn !
Its sweetest melodies arrest
   The angel song of seraphim ; .

They hold thy hymns, to them so new—
    These transports of thy human love—
Most worthy to give praises due
    To Father, Word, and Heavenly Dove.

The syren world, with artful skill,
    Its votaries may captivate,—
And pleasant is the secret thrill
    Which waves or forest winds create;
But art and nature must be mute,
    When Mary, Queen of heavenly choirs,
Within the Temple strikes her lute,
    And sings the hymns which God inspires.

May that sweet voice direct and guide
    Through life my spirit's tranquil course!
That music charm it—make it glide
    In peace unto the heavenly source!
May I in undersong repeat,
    With humble love, the sacred hymn,
And finish, at our Saviour's Feet,
    This blissful task of praising Him.

VI.

THE GOD OF MARY.

> *Whithersoever thou shalt go, I will go: and where thou shalt dwell, I also will dwell. Thy people shall be my people, and thy God my God.* RUTH i. 16.

O GOD of Mary, Thine own Hands
  Which made her, also fashioned me;
  And if her gifts, received from Thee,
Allured Thee to these desert lands—
    O Mary's God,
      Art Thou not mine?
      My Love Divine!
      My heart's Abode!

Art Thou less powerful, or less great
  In what Thou hast performed for me?
  Or am I less Thy work than She?
Thou lovest all Thou dost create.

O Mary's God!
　　Art Thou not mine?
　　My Love Divine!
My heart's Abode!

One Beauty do not all behold?
　One Wisdom do not all explore?
　One Goodness do not all adore?
Does not one Love all souls enfold?
　　O Mary's God!
　　　Art Thou not mine?
　　　My Love Divine!
　　My heart's Abode!

Though I have fewer gifts received,
　Though sick and weary be my head—
　To me "I pardon thee" is said,
And Thou more sufferings hast relieved.
　　O Mary's God!
　　　Art Thou not mine?
　　　My Love Divine!
　　My heart's Abode!

Nay, measureless in Charity,
  Thou didst at last give even her!
  Divine contrivance! to confer
Thy perfect gifts in her on me.
    O Mary's God!
      Art thou not mine?
      My Love Divine!
      My heart's Abode!

And if our gifts appear but small,
  Her greater ones were for a sign,
  And promise of that Love Divine
Which gives Itself entire to all.
    O Mary's God!
      Art Thou not mine?
      My Love Divine!
      My heart's Abode!

Yes, in the Eucharistic Feast,
  Thy greatest gift!—the Living Bread,
  With which her happy soul was fed,
Refreshes me, who am the least.

O Mary's God!
   Art Thou not mine?
   My Love Divine!
My heart's Abode!

And when my exile here is o'er,
   Good things shall fill my soul above,
   Glad torrents of true life and love
In Thee with her for evermore.
   O Mary's God!
      Art Thou not mine?
      My Love Divine!
   My heart's Abode!

VII.

MARY A REVELATION OF GOD.

> *She is the brightness of eternal light, and the unspotted mirror of God's majesty, and the image of His goodness.* Wis. vii. 26.

Did I hear the angels singing
   In the star-land wilderness,
Did I hear the heavens ringing
   With God's praise—I should learn less
Of His Grandeur and His Splendour,
   Than I learn from Mary's Heart,
With its vast love, strong and tender—
   Oh my God how great Thou art!

At His tread, the lofty mountain
   Trembles; but all-motionless,
Clear and still, this crystal fountain
   Mirrors all His Loveliness.

Quiet as the sea at even,
  When the sun sinks down to rest,
Mary's soul shines soft as heaven,
  When God hides in her pure breast.

Full of thorns and demon-haunted,
  Earth lay long a desert waste,
Until Jesse's Rod was planted,
  . Mary, chastest of the chaste—
To her, by the Spirit wafted,
  Came the Flower of Paradise;
And the Rod bloomed, though ingrafted
  On a stock that sins and dies.

When we see Our Lady kneeling
  In a trembling, humble prayer,
To God's clemency appealing
  To be merciful and spare—
Angels with their thrice sung "Holy"
  Of His justice tell us less,
Than does Mary, suppliant, lowly,
  Worshipping His Holiness.

Sweet art Thou, O God of Mary,
   "Taste and see," is Thy sweet call
In Thy heavenly Sanctuary,
   All to her, and All to all—
Like her, loving as a mother—
   Having all loves in Thy Heart—
Father, Spouse, Child, Sister, Brother,
   O my God! how Sweet Thou art.

VIII.

THE AVOWAL OF ST. BERNARDINE OF SIENA.

> *Her have I loved, and have sought her out from my youth, and have desired to take her for my spouse, and I became a lover of her beauty.* WIS. viii. 2.

My heart is not mine any longer,
   I confess it to you, dearest friends;
I love, and no love could be stronger,
   For my Loved One the whole world transcends—
My heart is not mine any longer!

'Tis useless to dwell on her beauty,
   She has utterly conquer'd my heart—
To praise her I feel is my duty,
   But her fairness excels all my art—
'Tis useless to dwell on her beauty.

I cannot endure life without her,
  Nor the length of the night and the day—
'Tis life to be thinking about her,
  So I love her, and live in that way—
I cannot endure life without her!

My study is only to find her—
  Unto this all my powers are trained;
My hope is that she will be kinder,
  My mind and my will are enchained—
My study is only to find her!

For her, then, my whole soul is yearning—
  After God, she has won all my love:
'Tis a bright and pure flame ever burning,
  'Tis a true vow recorded above—
For her then my whole soul is yearning!

So now, need I name this fair Maiden,
  And say, Mary the Mother of God?
My bosom at last is unladen—
  She should have every drop of my blood!
So now, need I name this fair Maiden?

IX.

AVE MARIA.

> *Mary was troubled at this saying, and thought within herself what manner of salutation this should be.* ST. LUKE i. 29.

LIKE a bright sunbeam, on its road
   Through sullen clouds with cheerful smile,
An echo in earth's dark abode
   Has spread joy through each gloomy aisle—
Those angel words in which we pray,
And sing to Mary every day
      Ave Maria,
      Gratia plena.

O sacred words! His message charms
   The Seraph of Eternal Love;
He soothes the innocent alarms
   Of Israel's fluttered, timid dove,

Her purest heart God asked for home,
Abhorring not that virgin womb.
    Ave Maria,
    Gratia plena.

Sweet words of love! in heaven sung
  Upon the glad Assumption day,
The angels' welcome, as they hung
  Above their Queen's triumphal way—
Words more harmonious could not be
In their immortal symphony.
    Ave Maria,
    Gratia plena.

The Holy Spirit aided them,
  More joyful song they never made,
Her Jesus held a diadem
  With flashing jewels all inlaid—
He crowned his Mother: Happy Son!
And led her to the Father's throne.
    Ave Maria,
    Gratia plena.

THE MAY CHAPLET.

The Ave is the prayer of all,
  Of virgin, with her shining lamp,
When summoned by the Bridegroom's call,
  The watchword of the Christian camp,
The praise of lisping infancy,
The hymn of all who hope in thee—
    Ave Maria,
    Gratia plena.

And may I thus my voice employ,
  O Queen ! O Mother of fair love !
O may it be my greatest joy
  To join the angel's song above,
And send one murmuring wavelet more
To praise thee on the eternal shore !
    Ave Maria,
    Gratia plena.

X.

CHRISTMAS AND COMMUNION.

> *They found Joseph and Mary,*
> *and the Infant lying in a manger.*
> LUKE ii. 16.

JESUS is in my heart—Archangels, as of old
  Ye knelt at Bethlehem, now adore in circling throng;
In helpless want, in bitter cold,
  He waits your worship and your song.

Against a frozen world's neglect and scornful slight,
  How poor the shelter of a cheerless heart like mine !
How sullen and how black the night
  Which frowns on Thee, O Guest divine !

Mary, too humble to disdain the lowly cave,
   For thy Son's sake do not a wretched heart despise;
Pity, great Queen, a suppliant slave,
   And make a stable Paradise.

Lend me thy heart, thy heart with flames of love,
   Hide from His sight the gloom of this sad realm;
Soul of our souls, come from above,
   And make each heart a Bethlehem.

XI.

THE HEAVENLY SAMARITAN.

> *A certain man fell among robbers, who also stripped him, and having wounded him, went away leaving him half dead. But a certain Samaritan being on his journey, came near him, and seeing him, was moved with compassion; and going up to him, bound up his wounds, pouring in oil and wine.* LUKE x. 30.

My careless soul in search of pleasures,
  From flower to flower unheeding strayed;
Her foes prepared their crafty measures—
  She fell into the ambuscade.
    Of treasure they bereft her,
    And well-nigh dead they left her,
  Poor wretch! too weak to call for aid.

In deadly swoon behold her lying,
   Laid low in this most piteous plight,
Those heavy eyelids, vainly trying
   To bear the excruciating light.
      One livid wound all over,
        With scarce a rag to cover
   Her hurts, and hide the sickening sight.

The eye of Mary soon was turning
   To where I had been roughly tost—
Her heart with love and mercy yearning,
   Or else for ever was I lost.
      Yes; had she not been near me,
      Had she delayed to hear me,
Salvation would have been the cost.

O gentle hands, so full of healing!
   O sweetest eyes! There comes a calm,
And o'er me, Mother, sleep is stealing,

Like the soft shadow from a palm !
  Thy tears soothe all our sadness,
  Thy dear voice brings back gladness—
Of broken hearts thou hope and balm !

O dear Samaritan ! descending
  From heavenly lands, thou bringest me
The new wine of the life unending,
  The healing oil of charity—
    The wine which doth refresh us
    Is Blood divine and precious,
  Shed for our sins on Calvary.

Bathe, bathe my soul, O heavenly Stranger,
  With that redeeming, sacred Wine !
It saves us in the hour of danger,
  It is our remedy divine—
    It cleanseth our offences,
    'Tis fragrance to our senses,
  O pour it on this heart of mine !

XII.

THE DREAM OF ST. KATHERINE.

> *I will espouse thee to me in justice and judgment, and in mercy, and in commiserations.* OSEE ii. 19.

O FAIREST Mother, ever young!
    Whose Son the ages make not old,—
O listen to my faltering tongue,
    And let me thy sweet Jesus hold!
Ah! let me taste the rapturous bliss
    Which made thy gentle bosom glow,—
And cover, with caressing kiss,
    His Feet, His Hands, His Sacred Brow.

Alas! He shudders at my sight—
    How stern and menacing His eyes!
They dart forth rays of searching light,
    Which show my soul her miseries;

She sees that she is Satan's prey—
  That unclean spirits in her dwell—
Who crouch, and lurk, and fiercely bay
  For carnage, savage hounds of hell.

O Holy Child, reject me not!
  To whom, Lord, can I go but Thee?
Thine eyes behold each sinful blot,
  And yet Thine arms must shelter me!
O flow, baptismal waters, flow!
  Repentance shall my sorrow prove—
O take the sin-stain from my brow,
  And make me worthy of His love!

O Lord! than thought itself more swift,
  Thou bringest to poor sinners grace;
The fallen penitent to lift,
  The soul's defilement to efface;

Great gifts Thy charity imparts,
    To change their need to rich estate—
Transformed by Thy sweet grace, their hearts
    Thy beauty makes inebriate.

How gentle, Mary, is thy gaze!
    It thrills me now with happiness,
My soul expands beneath the rays
    Of thy surpassing tenderness.
O now, if I might but embrace
    The Infant Jesus in my arms,
He would not turn away His face,
    Nor cause again those dread alarms!

O ecstasy! O sweet surprise!
    His little hands stretch out for me—
"I love thee!"—say those infant eyes—
    And I!—I burn with charity!
O soul of mine! weak foolish thing!—
    A bride of Jesus Christ thou art!
Receive thy Love's betrothal ring,
    And rest thee on His Sacred Heart!

XIII.

BENEDICTION AT NOTRE DAME DES VICTOIRES.

Ave verum Corpus natum de Maria Virgine.

ALL hail! Thou Image pure and sweet!
  With gentle smile a mother shows
The Child-God to the crowds who meet
  To share the blessing He bestows;
    O Mother, I implore thee,
      O Child, on Thee I call,
    Yes, Little One, adore Thee,
      My King, my Living God, my All.

O faultless sculpture! fairest sign
  Of sacred mysteries beneath!
That life-like loveliness of thine
  Seems from the Everlasting's breath!

O Mother, I implore thee,
   O Child, on Thee I call,
Yes, Little One, adore Thee,
   My King, my Living God, my All!

Thy silence has a thousand ways
   To captivate Thy votaries,
To blame their faults, to whisper praise—
   To call forth tears, to stay their sighs—
     O Mother, I implore Thee,
       O Child on Thee I call,
     Yes, Little One, adore Thee,
       My King, my Living God, my All!

O youthful acolythes! prepare
   The torches, incense, thurible,—
O priests of God, entone the prayer,
   And lead the joyous canticle.
     O Mother, I implore Thee,
       O Child, on Thee I call,
     Yes, Little One, adore Thee,
       My King, my Living God, my All!

O Heaven's Angels ! Ye of earth !
  Make every heart with fervour burn—
The shadow hath its priceless worth—
  But see the Substance in its turn !
    O Mother, I implore Thee,
      O Child, on Thee I call,
    Yes, Little One, adore Thee,
      My King, my Living God, my All !

O priest ! her Child is in thy hands,
  In thy place Mary seems to come—
In glory's light the Mother stands,
  And shows the Fruit of her chaste womb.
    O Mother, I implore Thee,
      O Child, on Thee I call,
    Yes, Little One, adore Thee,
      My King, my Living God, my All !

XIV.

THEY HAVE NO WINE.

' Thou hast kept the good wine until now. JOHN ii. 10.

How happy! at the nuptials of the Lamb,
    How happy Mary is! for she is Bride,
And Jesus Bridegroom, light, feast, cup of balm,
    All—to the Lov'd One at His side.

He is her Son, her Father, aye, her Love—
    And, whilst she leans her dear head on His breast,
She bids the angels of her court above
    Heed well the wishes of each guest.

THEY HAVE NO WINE.

O Mary! look on us from heaven's height—
    Far, far away in this life's banishment!
Assigned the lowest place, scarce in His sight—
    Can souls be happy and content?

We are athirst—whilst round us scoffers drain
    Their sinful cup, with impious discourse;
Weak fools! their mirth is false, their pleasure vain,
    The dregs are anguish and remorse.

We are athirst and heart-sick,—Ah! we need
    That Wine which doth repair life's daily loss,
And makes man in the ways of heaven speed,
    Strong with the folly of the Cross.

O plead our cause with that most tender Heart,
    With Him who oft was footsore on this earth;
Poor souls that droop—poor bleeding hearts that smart
    Must surely need some heavenly mirth.

O Mary's Angels ! ye, the Bridegroom's Friends !
   Fulfil her word, prepare to do His will !
The bitter water to the brim ascends—
   The cup of life our sorrows fill !

Dear Lord ! great God ! her eyes look unto Thine—
   Thou knowest the wish of her who gave Thee birth ;
Ah ! Thou dost change to Heaven's delicious wine,
   For Mary's sake, the tears of earth !

XV.

THE BLESSED SACRAMENT.

> *Wisdom hath mingled her wine, and set forth her table: she hath sent her maids to invite to the tower, and to the walls of the city. Whosoever is a little one let him come to me. Come, eat my bread, and drink the wine I have mingled for you.* PROV. ix. 1.

O HEAVENLY Virgin! the God of thy fathers,
  The God who, to save us, lay hid in thy womb—
Is here, and around Him mysteriously gathers
  The folds of Faith's veil, in His dear altar home;
    Queen of Heaven, lend unto me,
      Mother, that pure heart of thine;
    Let me worship with thee, through thee,
      Jesus hidden in this shrine!

'Tis He, whose sweet visit, and unspoken greeting,
  Awoke the Fore-runner to leap in strange glee;
When the Babes yet unborn heard thy sweet song repeating
  The marvels which God had accomplished in thee.
      Queen of Heaven, lend unto me,
        Mother, that pure heart of thine,
      Let me worship with thee, through thee,
        Jesus hidden in this shrine!

'Tis He, who beneath Sacramental appearance,
  Sought thy heart, His first home, as its heavenly Food—
Love breaks His own laws by divine interference,
  And his Friends eat with thee the Lord's Body and Blood.
      Queen of Heaven, lend unto me,
        Mother, that pure heart of thine;
      Let me worship with thee, through thee,
        Jesus hidden in this shrine!

O pure Grain of Wheat, bruised on Calvary's mountain,
  O Bread, made with fires of God's burning love!
O Blood of the wine-press! the Saviour's sweet Fountain—
  What transports of praise can our thankfulness prove?

Queen of Heaven, lend unto me,
   Mother, that pure heart of thine;
Let me worship with thee, through thee,
   Jesus hidden in this shrine!

'Tis He, the same Jesus, who in the poor manger,
   Gave Himself to the Magi—the shepherds—to all—
Thy silence still bids us approach the meek Stranger,
   Through thee, the Child's Mother, as at Bethle'm's stall.
      Queen of Heaven, lend unto me,
         Mother, that pure heart of thine;
      Let me worship with thee, through thee,
         Jesus hidden in this shrine!

'Tis He, who clung to thee, so sweetly caressing
   Thy virginal neck with divine loving arms,
Whom thou to thy bosom wert constantly pressing,
   With mother's bold love and with creature's alarms.
      Queen of Heaven, lend unto me,
         Mother, that pure heart of thine;
      Let me worship with thee, through thee,
         Jesus hidden in this shrine!

'Tis He, the dear God, whose ineffable brightness
   Surrounds thee, transfigured, and clothed with the sun ;
He delights in thy heart of immaculate whiteness,
   Which serves Him for altar, for incense, and throne.
      Queen of Heaven, lend unto me,
         Mother, that pure heart of thine,
      Let me worship with thee, through thee,
         Jesus hidden in this shrine !

XVI.

THE SEVEN DOLOURS.

> *And their own soul a sword shall pierce, that out of many hearts thoughts may be revealed.*
> LUKE ii. 35.

I.

WHEN Jesus on the altar of the Lord,
The willing victim of mankind was laid,
Thy heart was pierced, O Mother, with the sword,
    And saw the future then display'd—
It bled to see a countless, helpless host
Of children through inhuman monsters lost—
Children whom Jesus had from Satan wrung
    With Blood, with tears on Calvary—
I see thee mourn the ruin of the young—
O Queen of sorrows, let me weep with thee!

II.

The King of kings, who clothes the stars with light,
Enjoys no peace, not even in a cave—
His parents flee, and, at the dead of night—
    In foreign land the Child they save.
What has He done, that earth should prove unkind,
And that His beauteous Feet should only find
A desert pathway, thick with briar and thorn—
    A waste of drear sterility?
I see thee mourn this world of wicked scorn—
O Queen of sorrows, let me weep with thee!

III.

At least the Temple will its Lord receive,
    And offer incense, love, and gratitude—
The Priests and Ancients will His words believe,
    Nor prove contemptuous and rude—
How comes it, then, that thou didst never feel
Such fear and anguish o'er thy spirit steal,

As when, to teach the doctors, He abode
    In Salem three days secretly?
I see thee mourn the ministers of God—
O Queen of sorrows, let me weep with thee!

IV.

If Jesus comes in manhood's fairest strength,
And shows us all His wealth of tenderness,
Shall we accept our humble King at length?
    His heavenly wisdom shall we bless?
No—even thus He found but cruel hate—
Thou hast beheld thine Abel's mangled state,
When dragged by crowds to death with blows and jeers,
    The sport of their ferocity—
I see thee mourn our manhood's primest years—
O Queen of sorrows, let me weep with thee!

V.

And when the Lord upon the tree of shame
Atones for all mankind, and makes us free—

When thou dost offer souls His love and name
    In marriage upon Calvary—
From Him, our bleeding Spouse, how oft we hide,
And make the Wound yet larger in His Side!
Enticed away to sin by Satan's arts,
    The penance of the Cross we flee—
I see thee mourn our hardened guilty hearts—
O Queen of sorrows, let me weep with thee!

VI.

Our Jesus follows to the gates of death
The sinner still unhappily astray:
To save him, even at the latest breath,
    With Arms of love He bars the way.
O Mother, come with Jesus when we die,
With Him receive our contrite heart's last sigh!
The ocean of His goodness from His eyes
    Our sins will hide, and set us free—
I see thee mourn our death-bed agonies—
O Queen of sorrows, let me weep with thee!

VII.

Is there perpetual peace within the tomb?
In spite of Jesus, and His Heart, His pains,
His tears, His Precious Blood—alas! the doom
    Reveals in us some lingering stains—
A fire awaits us—slow, yet not for aye—
Fearful yet kind, it burns those stains away—
A hallowed remedy—yet, Mother, come,
    Appease God's just severity!
I see thee mourning o'er the Prison-home—
O Queen of sorrows—let me weep with thee!

XVII.

WOMAN BEHOLD THY SON!

> *When Jesus therefore had seen His mother and the disciple standing whom he loved, He saith to His mother: Woman, behold thy son. After that He saith to the disciple: Behold thy mother.* JOHN xix. 26.

I LIVE, and now not I, but Jesus lives in me;
O Mother of my Lord! I too become thy son!
In heaven the glorious King reveres and honours thee,
    On earth—this poorest one!

Yes, Jesus on the Cross proclaimed aloud His choice,
He left thee unto us before His bitter death—
He named thee mankind's Mother with uplifted voice,
    And with His latest breath.

For, miracle of love or miracle of might,
He speaks, and it is done—by Him all things are made;
He willed there should be light—and lo! there was the light—
    The Maker is obeyed.

"Woman, behold thy Son!" this gentle Jesus said,
"Behold thy Mother," next addressed to us was heard;
'Twas done—as into Flesh His sole word changes bread—
    He needs but speak the word.

Yes, Thou hast said it, Lord! but was it said for me?
Am I a Jesus, then? alas! my dearest Lord,
Can I be like thee? I! who know myself to be
    So guilty, so abhorr'd?

Am I a Jesus? I!—a Jesus without prayer,
Without a heart to love, without zeal, energy,
A sanctuary profaned, a mournful ruin, where
    Lurks nameless misery!

One look of Him I have—alas! that woful look,
When, loaded with our shame, the Lord came forth to die,
When, buffeted and scourged, the Man of Sorrows took
    The road to Calvary!

But 'tis no longer I! and never shall be so—
My Jesus succours me, and Mary aids my strife—
Their love supreme shall be the only rule I know,
    Their love shall be my life! . . . .

II.

Thy Heart, O Mother, is our Saviour's last bequest—
A nobler, worthier gift He had not to bestow—
And nobly hast thou loved, fulfilling His behest,
    The children of thy woe!

I take the precious gift—the sinner! whom Saint John
Did sadly represent upon that day of grace—
Thy heart adopted him who took thee to his own—
    O give me there a place!

Thou saidst unto him, "Come, thou Firstborn of my grief!
To the Last Supper Room—conduct thy Mother there—
My other Jesus! come, the soul has no relief
    For woe like ours but prayer."

"Come, Son and Priest, from whom I daily shall receive,
Throughout the rest of life, my sweetest Living Bread—
Thy first sad task must be to watch with me and grieve
    For that same Jesus dead!"

Thou, Mother, would'st all hearts in thy one heart could be,
To welcome that dear Lord, the Manna from above—
That all might be one throne, one heaven of purity,
    One canticle of love.

Oh! Mother, do not pause, perform thy blest desire,
Make body, soul and heart completely, only thine!
What in us is not Christ—O burn it, Sacred Fire!
    Consume it, Love Divine!

THE MAY CHAPLET.

XVIII.

THE BRIDE OF THE HOLY GHOST.

> *The fountain of gardens; the well of living waters, which run with a strong stream from Libanus.*
> CANTICLES iv. 15.

O TURN thy kind eyes on this desert of woe,
   Fair Bride of the Holy Spirit!
Thy grace, sweet as manna descending, bestow—
   The grace which thy sons inherit.

Come, thou virginal Spouse of the Spirit of Love,
   Come, Mother of Christ our Brother—
To the poor and the orphan descend from above—
   O come like the dew, sweet Mother!

THE BRIDE OF THE HOLY GHOST.

We will build thee a shrine in our innermost heart,
   Now clouded with secret sadness—
Thou wilt come—for no stranger to sorrow thou art—
   O bring to us holy gladness.

With thee labour is lighter, and varied with rest,
   And noon has its shadows grateful—
In earth's dark recesses where thou art a guest,
   Thy light makes the gloom less hateful.

If it were not for thee, who could quiet the fears
   Of the rescued from ways of folly?
But for thee, is there one who would dry all their tears,
   Or solace their melancholy?

Where thou comest, nor evil nor sorrow is seen—
   Our winter and frost are over—
Soon the barren and desolate land becomes green—
   Choice flowers our gardens cover.

All the wealth of thy Spouse is entrusted to thee—
   At thy knee thy poor children gather—
For the future, at least, let us innocent be
   In the Face of our Heavenly Father!

XIX.

BLESSEDNESS.

> *Yea rather, blessed are they who hear the word of God and keep it.*
> LUKE xi. 28.

SHALL I call blest the day that welcomed Mary's birth,
    The womb that bore th'Immaculate—
The air she breathed, the milk that nourished her, the hearth,
    Before she came—so desolate?

Shall I call blest the beams that flushed Aurora's face,
    When first she kissed this fairest Child—
Cison, and Endor's plain—whose flowers are said to trace
    The footsteps of the Undefiled?

Shall I call blest God's House, wherein the Maiden spent
  The lowly lot which was her choice—
Its courts and turtle doves, its echoes sweetly blent
  With the soft music of her voice?

Shall I call blest the tomb, the fragrant tomb that kept
  God's fairest Flower, when life was o'er,
For those three days wherein the Mother-maiden slept—
  Then gave her back for evermore?

I will call blest the soul, that sleeps in calm repose
  Beneath the mantle of her love—
And ever breathes its love far sweeter than the rose
  Distilling fragrances above!

XX.

WHERE MUST WE SEEK OUR MOTHER.

> *Wisdom is easily seen by them that love her and is found by them that seek her. She preventeth them that covet her, so that she first sheweth herself unto them.* WISDOM vi. 13.

WHERE must we seek our Mother blest?
Which echo question with her name?
May only angels reach her rest,
As when of yore Saint Gabriel came?
Must earth be left on pinion bold,
To pacify this sense of loss?
Or is her place of dwelling told
To none but desert saint grown old
   In service of the Cross?

The saints invoke this Heavenly Queen
In storms, and when calm comes again,
In city square, on village green—
In every joy and every pain.

Yes, he who loves her everywhere
Believes and feels that she is nigh,
That on hell's brink none need despair,
For she can rescue with her prayer
   The sinner ere he die.

Her life throughout the unseen world
Has stretched, and broadened like the sea—
On Lucifer from heaven hurl'd
Her footprint shows triumphantly.
But, Mary, on the prayerful heart,
Which glows with fires of holy love,
Bright shines the grace thou dost impart,
And teaches, Mother, where thou art—
   God's gifts thy presence prove.

But, Mary, at some favourite shrine
My heart loves most to seek for thee,
Where murmured Aves mix with mine,
And hidden saints tell beads with me—

At thy dear shrines proud scorners jest;
But how I love to find them spread
Throughout the world, from east to west,
Where'er the land with Faith is blest,
    And God is honouréd!

All hail, sweet refuges, all hail!
Fair gardens of virginity!
Calm havens! whence our souls make sail
To reach the land beyond the sea.
Hail, woodland chapels of our Queen!
Where sanctity pervades the air—
Love thanks you for your friendly screen,
For love delights to breathe unseen
    The prayer which brings her there!

Our soul will bid farewell to Faith,
Her guide, great Queen, in seeking thee—
The day she is set free by death—
The Day when face to face we see!

Then, midst the countless company
Attendant at thy starry throne,
Her blissful lot shall ever be
To join the angels' harmony,
　And bless thee with thy Son.

XXI.

VIRGO PRUDENTISSIMA.

Prudentes virgines, aptate vestras lampades: ecce sponsus venit exite obviam ei. ANT. COM. VIRG.

'TIS late, and o'er the earth night's shadowy pall
  Hath fallen, colder than the dew,
  To hide hearts colder still—and through
The hours I wait, and listen for the call :
    Rise, virgins, quickly rise !
      The King ye serve draws near !
      The God ye love is here—
  Make haste, be wise, be wise !

O welcome cry ! by herald angels made !
  Ring out above the tempest's moan !
  I wait here wearily alone—
My summons to depart is long delay'd !

Rise, virgins, quickly rise !
   The King ye serve draws near !
   The God ye love is here—
Make haste, be wise, be wise !

Yet is my soul prepared to meet her Lord ?
  Has she the virgin's bridal light ?
  Has she the garment pure and white ?
Ah! who can tell? And hark! I hear the word:
   Rise, virgins, quickly rise !
      The King ye serve draws near !
      The God ye love is here—
   Make haste, be wise, be wise !

Most wise of virgins ! Lily amongst thorns !
  Are any wise except for thee?
  The prudence of thy charity,
In that last hour, each righteous soul adorns.
   Rise, virgins, quickly rise!
      The King ye serve draws near !
      The God ye love is here—
   Make haste, be wise, be wise !

My lamp burns low—oh, give me of thine oil!
  Give! for the time doth still suffice.
  Give! without money, without price,
The wedding garment washed from every soil.
    Rise, virgins, quickly rise!
      The King ye serve draws near!
      The God ye love is here—
    Make haste, be wise, be wise!

O bless thee! Oil most fragrant and most pure
  Thy thoughtful, tender love bestows!
  The lamp is trimmed, and brightly glows—
Its shining makes the midnight road secure.
    Rise, virgins, quickly rise!
      The King ye serve draws near!
      The God ye love is here—
    Make haste, be wise, be wise!

O Virgin Mother! sinner as I am,
  Beneath thy mantle let me hide,
  Until my soul is beautified,
And covered with the white wool of thy Lamb!

Rise, virgins, quickly rise!
 The King ye serve is near—
 The God ye love is here—
Make haste, be wise, be wise!

Most Prudent Virgin! what, alas! have I
 To offer thee? What pearl to give?
 For thy sake, ever, whilst I live
On this dark earth, I'll spread the midnight cry
 Rise, virgins, quickly rise!
 The King ye serve is near—
 The God ye love is here—
 Make haste, be wise, be wise!

XXII.

THE PROCESSION OF VIRGINS.

> *After her shall virgins be brought to the king, her neighbours shall be brought to thee. They shall be brought with gladness and rejoicing, they shall be brought into the temple of the king.* Ps. xliv. 15.

HARK! David sings in deathless strain
  The glad lot that befalls us;
Our Queen leads on her virgin train—
  And to the Temple calls us.
     Happy bridesmaids, prepare!
     To the nuptials repair!
     Sing in echo's charmed ear:
     We are here! we are here!

THE MAY CHAPLET.

How beautiful, how fair our Queen !
  Our King, how sweet and tender !
The gentle virtues in her seen
  Have won the King of splendour.
      And our souls in her track
      Tarry not, nor look back,
      But leave all earth holds dear ;
      We are here ! we are here !

They are not tuneful seraphim,
  But virgins that are singing ;
'Tis their new song, the Bridal Hymn,
  That through the sky is ringing.
      Ah ! more fragrant and sweet
      Than the rose 'neath her feet,
      Heaven's Queen draweth near;
      We are here ! we are here !

Alas ! can our poor voices be
  With virgin voice united—
With those whose love triumphantly
  Unto the Lamb is plighted?

O Divine Lamb of God!
Cleanse our souls with Thy Blood!
And we'll sing without fear:
We are here! we are here!

XXIII.

HYMN OF LOVE.

Love is strong as death. CAN-
TICLES viii. 7.

LOVE, ever love—as God ordains,
   Yes, love the things that are above—
The love whose bitterness remains
   Shall not receive the name of love.
Go, seek the land where Mary reigns,
   Fly thither, hearts, on wing of dove—
     Love then, with love that never dies,
     With love the Sacred Heart will bless,
        And so be wise
        In happiness.

Love, ever love what God bestowed
  On His Divine and Only Son,
A Mother—Ah, what love He showed !
  How tenderly He placed the crown
Upon her brow, in heaven's abode,
  Whilst Paradise in bliss looked on.
    Love then, with love that never dies,
    With love the Sacred Heart will bless,
        And so be wise
        In happiness.

Love, ever love, with love intense !
  No seraph's transport can compare
Unto that charity immense
  In which our Mother took a share—
Which counted not the vast expense,
  But died to free us from despair.
    Love then, with love that never dies,
    With love the Sacred Heart will bless,
        And so be wise
        In happiness.

Love, ever love—'tis her reward!
  She asks none else for all she bore—
Ah! think, she must have found it hard
  So long to nurse the sick and sore—
Her own departure to retard,
  To be our Mother more and more!
    Love then, with love that never dies,
    With love the Sacred Heart will bless,
      And so be wise
      In happiness.

Love, ever love—it is her right!
  Then, after Jesus, give her all—
Her beauty, goodness shine so bright,
  Her charms our pining hearts enthrall.
Great Queen, admit us to thy sight,
  We listen for the welcome call!
    Love then, with love that never dies,
    With love the Sacred Heart will bless,
      And so be wise
      In happiness.

Love, ever love—around one hearth
   In love form one fraternal ring—
One Mother to us all gave birth
   In Christ, our Brother and our King.
Ah, then, let all in heaven on earth
   One hymn of love to Mary sing!
     Love then, with love that never dies,
     With love the Sacred Heart will bless,
        And so be wise
        In happiness.

THE MAY CHAPLET.

XXIV.

SHOW THY FACE.

> *Show me thy face, let thy voice sound in my ears: for thy voice is sweet, and thy face comely.* CANTICLES ii. 14.

An eastern radiance crowns her brow,
   And lustrous is her dark hair's braid,
A gentle glance her eyes bestow,
   And kinder lips have never prayed—
Ah! nobly doth her beauty show
   The grace that fills the Mother-maid.
     Mother blest! show thy face,
       Deign thy veil to remove!
     On our hearts let us trace
       The dear features we love!

SHOW THY FACE.

We are impatient to behold
    Thy features lit with glory's light—
That heavenly look, wherein is told
    Thy history since the Christmas night
When, Mother, thou didst dare enfold
    In sheltering arms the God of might.
        Mother blest ! show thy face,
            Deign thy veil to remove !
        On our hearts let us trace
            The dear features we love !

O wherefore, wherefore thus conceal
    A vision holy and divine ?
Receive our suppliant appeal,
    And let thy face upon us shine !
What truth, what love it would reveal !
    Sweet Mother, to our prayer incline !
        Mother blest ! show thy face,
            Deign thy veil to remove !
        On our hearts let us trace
            The dear features we love !

There would we worship innocence,
    Simplicity and modesty—
And sweetness, courage, penitence—
    There truest wisdom learn from thee—
For in thy lovely countenance,
    Fair Mother, every grace we see!
        Mother blest! show thy face,
            Deign thy veil to remove!
        On our hearts let us trace
            The dear features we love!

What happiness the Blessed feel!
    Who on that face for ever gaze;
They see the likeness, as they kneel,
    Unto thy Jesus, whom they praise;
They see Him shine, put as a seal
    Upon thy heart, for endless days!
        Mother blest! show thy face,
            Deign thy veil to remove!
        On our hearts let us trace
            The dear features we love!

XXV.

REVELATRIX.

> *I am the mother of fair love, and of fear, and of knowledge, and of holy hope.* ECCLESIASTICUS xxiv. 24.

WHO shall declare the deep abyss of might,
The riches, the magnificence, the height
Of God the Father, whom the heavens bless?
 Tis thine, the Angels' Queen,
 To tell all thou hast seen,
Thou mirror of supernal loveliness.

Who shall declare His Wisdom's festal call,
The torrent of delights, the banquet hall
Of God the Son, His Word, the Light of Light?
 Tis thine, Light's undefiled
 True Mother and true Child,
To shed rays of that glory on our night.

Who shall declare the all-consuming fires,
The strong sweet love, the jubilant desires
Of God the Holy Ghost, the Heavenly Dove?
  Tis thine—to whom He came,
  The Breath! The Living Flame!
To kindle in our souls His fires of love.

Who shall declare how fell celestial Dew
This barren world to fertilise anew—
How God vouchsafed to come from heaven to earth?
  Tis thine—sweet Mother-maid!
  Fair Flower! that ne'er shall fade,
The Spirit's Bride! to tell us of Christ's Birth.

Who shall declare the secrets of that Heart,
So meek and humble, burning to impart
To all Its boundless wealth of love and grace?
  'Tis thine—Its Confidante,
  To know His love, our want—
And lead the poor before His Blessed Face.

Who shall declare the royal recompense,
The sweet repose, the happiness immense
Prepared for those who love and serve their God?
    'Tis thine, who shinest bright,
      Like ivory in God's light—
To guide us safely to that Blest Abode!

THE MAY CHAPLET.

XXVI.

THE VISION OF S. PHILIP.

> *I love them that love me: and they that in the morning early shall watch for me, shall find me.* PROV. viii. 17.

HE that desires aught but Thee,
   O Lord, is led by error—
Who loves Thee not falls shamefully,
   A ruin and a terror.
Come, Mother, to me in my pain,
   Would I could give some token
Of love, and sing thy praise! 'Tis vain!
   The harp is mute and broken.
     Receive my dying breath,
        Madonna mia!
     Life, Sweetness, Hope in death,
        Maria!

I die... Ah Mother!—is it thou?
  Madonna blest, and dearest!
And art thou come to see me now?
  How gentle thou appearest!
And art thou here to take me home,
  Or drive away my fever?
If I get well, shall I become
    More faithful? I fear, never!
      Receive my dying breath,
        Madonna mia!
      Life, Sweetness, Hope in death,
        Maria!

Most beautiful in purity!
  Most beautiful in splendour!
Most beautiful in all I see!
  My Queen, my sweet defender!
Ah! let me press unto my heart
  Thy robe of azure glory,
So let my happy soul depart,
  Whilst thou art bending o'er me!

THE MAY CHAPLET.

>   Receive my dying breath,
>   Madonna mia!
>   Life, Sweetness, Hope in death,
>   Maria!

To die ... to die ... in thy dear sight—
  In thy sight to awaken!
Make haste my soul, now take thy flight,
  This earth must be forsaken!
But no—God's will, that leaves me here,
  To love I must endeavour,
And live—that death may be more dear,
  More beautiful than ever!
>   Receive my dying breath,
>   Madonna mia!
>   Life, Sweetness, Hope in death,
>   Maria!

XXVII.

OUR LADY OF THE MIRACULOUS MEDAL.

Put me as a seal upon thy heart, as a seal upon thy arm. CANT. viii. 6.

UNTO the Father,
  When life was done,
Christ led His Mother,
  Claiming her crown.
Yet she remained not
  In that far light—
Cloud-like she hovers
  Ever in sight.
    Hail Queen of Heaven!
    Dawn of the day!
    Bright Star of Even!
    Lighten our way!

THE MAY CHAPLET.

Flinging down fragrance,
   Scents of the Spring,
Rising like incense,
   Ring over ring,
On the Moon's pavement
   Shining she stands—
And Ocean to greet her
   Lifts up his hands.
        Hail Queen of Heaven!
        Dawn of the Day!
        Bright Star of Even!
        Lighten our way!

Golden in splendour,
   Dazzling and rare—
Meek in her greatness,
   Gentle and fair.
Heaven such beauty
   Never has seen,
Vision of gladness!
   Bright and serene.

Hail Queen of Heaven!
Dawn of the day!
Bright Star of Even!
Lighten our way!

From her hands diamond
  Dew-drops are shed,
Like the rubies which Jesus
  Gave when He bled.
Her crown grows the brighter
  As the Saints come,
The crowd of the Blessed
  Blesses her womb.
      Hail Queen of Heaven!
      Dawn of the Day!
      Bright Star of Even!
      Lighten our way!

Mary! my soul calls
  On thy dear name;
Build there thine altar,
  Kindle thy flame.

THE MAY CHAPLET.

Glow on my bosom,
  God's seal and sign—
Bright golden treasure
  Sigil divine !
      Hail Queen of Heaven !
        Dawn of the day !
      Bright Star of Even !
        Lighten our way !

In the night's tempest,
  Be thou my light !
If the snake strike me,
  Heal thou his bite !
Thine it is ever
  Satan to crush—
Thine my heart's tempest,
  Mother, to hush !
      Hail Queen of Heaven !
        Dawn of the Day !
      Bright Star of Even !
        Lighten our way !

XXVIII.

SPEAK TO MY HEART.

> *Thou that dwellest in the gardens, the friends hearken: make me hear thy voice.* CANTICLES viii. 13.

O thou, whose voice God's Word calls sweet—
   At which His Heart rejoices,
When all His Saints and Angels meet
   To praise Him with their voices—
O wilt thou let thy voice be heard
   By hearts that are sin-laden?
Speak to my heart one only word—
   O speak, sweet Mother-maiden.

'Tis said, that men of holiness
   To thy dear speech are bidden—
That many a simple shepherdess
   Has talked to thee, unchidden—

To one—that hath an ear to hear,
    Whose gathering tear-drops glisten--
Speak to my heart, O mother dear,
    And let thy poor child listen!

O sweetest voice, O sweetest sound!
    What miracles it worketh—
Whether the outward sense is bound,
    Or in the soul it lurketh!
Its accents opened heaven's gate,
    Made heaven's King our Brother—
Speak to my heart, Immaculate!
    O speak to me, my Mother.

The language of the world seems sweet,
    Just as its false things glitter;
With deadly poison 'tis replete,
    And gall is not more bitter.
There pride and jealousy are sown,
    There hatred's worst incentive—
Speak to my heart, speak thou alone,
    Thy servant is attentive.

SPEAK TO MY HEART.

'Tis true thy voice inflicts its wound—
   It has its accents burning—
But hearts are thus to love attuned,
   On fire with holiest yearning—
Thy little ones true wisdom learn,—
   The old again feel youthful—
Speak to my heart, then, in its turn,
   O make it pure and truthful.

O echo of the Saviour's voice,
   In tones so soft and lowly!
Thy music is my joy, my choice,
   Thou sweetness of the Holy!
When "Share the gladness of thy Lord"
   Unto my soul is spoken,
Speak to my heart the same blest word,
   Yet keep the heart unbroken!

XXIX.

THE SERVANT OF MARY.

> *She shall not fear for her house in the cold of snow: for all her domestics are clothed with double garments.* PROV. xxxi. 21.

SERVANT of thine, O Mary, feels no shame—
    Flower-crown'd
    And renown'd.
Mother of God, 'tis service but in name—
    Serving thee,
    I am free!
Virgin most wise
    Rule me and teach!
True wisdom lies
    In thy sweet speech!

To serve the world is blindest wilfulness—
    All is vain,
    All is pain;
But we thy service more and more can bless—
    Here we gain,
    And we reign.
  Virgin most wise
    Rule me and teach!
  True wisdom lies
    In thy sweet speech!

Thy sacred images I love to kiss,
    Till thy light
    Greet my sight.
To wear thy livery night and day is bliss,
    For my love
    Thus I prove.
  Virgin most wise
    Rule me and teach!
  True wisdom lies
    In thy sweet speech!

These holy scapulars I love to kiss,
      And to keep
      During sleep.
Thy beads, like Philip, I would never miss,
      Dearest bands!
      From my hands.
    Virgin most wise
      Rule me and teach!
    True wisdom lies
      In thy sweet speech!

O can I ever give thee service due?
      Gifts are shared,
      Faults are spared—
'Twere just, instead of crosses light and few—
      If I bore
      Thousands more.
    Virgin most wise
      Rule me and teach!
    True wisdom lies
      In thy sweet speech!

Thy goodness were content, if we but strove
>   For desire,
>   And more fire,
A little patience, and exceeding love,
>   With its dart
>   In the heart.
>   Virgin most wise
>   Rule me and teach!
>   True wisdom lies
>   In thy sweet speech!

Two precepts bind all souls beneath thy sway—
>   Holy life,
>   Love, not strife.
Thy tender smile illumes the happy way
>   Of the blest
>   To their rest!
>   Virgin most wise
>   Rule me and teach!
>   True wisdom lies
>   In thy sweet speech!

XXX.

INTERCEDE.

> *Now therefore pray for us, for thou art a holy woman, and one fearing God.* JUDITH viii. 29.

IF we wander like sheep, and our souls fall a prey
   To the wolf of the desert, that prowls where they feed,—
If Jesus at last leaves them lost and astray—
   O Mother of Mercy, do thou intercede!

If, a thousand times pardoned, we still dare offend,
   And try Divine patience and love, without heed
That the gentle forbearance in vengeance must end—
   O Mother of Mercy, do thou intercede!

INTERCEDE.

If our sin-blinded soul cannot find in the gloom
    The Fountain of Jesus, the Five Wounds that bleed,
The fair Tree of Life, the sweet Fruit of thy womb—
    O Mother of Mercy, do thou intercede!

If, naked and poor, we will utter no prayer,
    Too proud to acknowledge our guilt and our need,
And fiercely determine to die in despair—
    O Mother of Mercy, do thou intercede!

If, broken and shipwrecked, we drift on life's tide,
    While Heaven and Hell on our doom seem agreed—
Heaven's gate shut so fast, and Hell's jaws stretched so wide—
    O Mother of Mercy, do thou intercede!

When pale death has grasped us with firm icy hold,
    That freezes the heart's blood, the brow's clammy bead,
And even the "Jesus!" on lips dead and cold—
    O Mother of Mercy, do thou intercede!

When feeble, worn out, in the dead of the night,
 The Bridegroom approaching, O how shall we speed?
With no wedding garment, no beauty, no light—
 O Mother of Mercy, do thou intercede!

When called to the judgment our soul learns its fate,
 And absence from God and from thee is decreed,
Till fitted by fire for Heaven's pure state—
 O Mother of Mercy, do thou intercede!

XXXI.

VENI CORONABERIS.

> *Then shall the king say to them that shall be on his right hand; Come ye blessed of my Father, possess you the kingdom prepared for you from the foundation of the world.* MATTHEW xxv. 34.

Day of alarm, day of supremest glory,
   Of awful majesty and light,
When Christ the Judge shall come to close earth's story,
   And show His justice and His might.

With Jesus on the clouds of heaven descending,
   O Mary, thou wilt re-appear;
His words to thee will be the thrilling ending
   Of those the happy just will hear.

"Come, O My Mother, and My brethren's Mother,
    Come to My Father's blessedness—
Already He has blessed thee as no other,
    And for My sake again will bless!

"When to the earth I came an unknown Stranger,
    Within thy heart was I received;
And thou didst clothe Me naked in the manger
    With raiment thine own hands had weaved.

"Thy Child—I hungered in this human nature,
    And thou wert all solicitude;
Thy Maker thirsted—begged from His own creature,
    Thy breast, My Mother, gave Me food.

"When love revealed Me as the Man of Sorrow,
    And I went forth in Pilate's chains,
Thou, weeping o'er Me, mournfully didst follow,
    Thy heart claimed part in all My pains.

"Come to receive thy living crown of merit—
    Thy joy, thy crown, these Saints shall be—
The Bridal Present of the Holy Spirit,
    His work on earth, His gift to thee." . . .

O make us thine, lest Christ the Lord reject us,
    The day His light shall search us through—
So wilt thou shield thy children, so protect us,
    Great Queen, beneath thy mantle blue!

The Wheat, which God into His barn shall gather,
    Is gleaned upon His Mother's path—
And thus all generations with the Father
    Shall bless her on the day of wrath!

ORIGINAL POEMS.

The Seven Dolours.

I.

THE PROPHECY OF S. SIMEON.

Lift from the manger the Holy One born of thee—
  Joseph hath all things prepared for the road—
Lowliest Mother, men ask, Is the stable free?
  Let the ox feed from the Cradle of God.

Angels sent Shepherds to visit thy hiding place,
  Jacob's star shewed the Three Kings thy retreat—
Saints pray in Sion, who pine for thy Infant's Face,
  Hoping to bless Him, and die at His Feet.

Fragments of Hebron's and Bethlehem's melodies
Wafted to Sion awaken her heart:
Echoes have stirred holy Simeon's memories,
Waiting the sign that shall bid him depart.

No law exists, made for thee and thy Little One,
Bidding thee hide in the shade of the Cave;
Leave thy device of love—forty full days are done,
Pity the world which thy Babe is to save.

See! Mary listens, and brings forth the Light of Lights,
Shining so softly, asleep in her arms—
Rays that erst dazzled the terrified Israelites
Beam on a bosom that feels no alarms.

Longed for and sought for, He comes to the Temple gate—
Lord God of hosts! are His heralds unheard?
Do not the Princes, the High Priest and Ancients wait,
Open their portals—and worship the Word?

THE PROPHECY OF ST. SIMEON.

Only Saint Simeon, he whom the Spirit led,
Waits for them, and for his long-promised grace,
Welcomes them, blesses them, bends low his hoary head,
Then takes the Babe in his trembling embrace.

Lo! a strange pallor has spread over Simeon's face,
Kissing his Lord's Feet, he thought to find death—
Spirit-stirred, now he must speak in the Holy Place
Stern words of woe with his weak falt'ring breath.

"He shall be set as a sign men shall contradict,
Dooms by this Child shall for ever be sealed—
In thine own soul shall the keen piercing sword inflict
Wounds at which hearts will grieve, thoughts be revealed!"

Mary then offers the young of the turtle dove,
Clasps to her bosom its Treasure again—
Pressing so closely, so deeply the Sword of Love
Into her heart with its exquisite pain. . . .

Sorrow may come, yet my soul do not hesitate,
'Tis but His shadow whom thou dost well love—
Safer is sorrow for man in his fallen state—
Bliss without pain we must look for Above.

II.

THE FLIGHT INTO EGYPT.

Her well-hidden nest is watched o'er by the bird;
The hind haunts the thicket where, far from the herd,
Her fawn lies concealed safely sheltered from harm,
Whilst out on the smooth lawn she feels no alarm—
But dearer thy home, gentle Mother! to thee—
Hid 'midst the lone hills of the green Galilee;
So secret the village, men well might suppose
The valley holds only the lily and rose—
   To thy home
   Neighbours come,
And behold the tiny Treasure—
   That God gave
   In Bethlehem's cave,
Jubilant with holy pleasure.

Around roam the flocks on the warm grassy hills,
The lambs lie about by their flower-girt rills,
The vineyards with fig-tree, grey olive and vine,
Make foliage to shade that sweet Flower of thine—
Saint Joseph keeps near at his work through the day,
And Angels' white wings may be heard on the way—
Profound as the peace in the realms whence they come
Is that which reigns here in the Nazarene home—
   Ah, beware
   Mother fair!
Hidden nests are sometimes harried—
   And the fawn
   By the lawn
From his mother oft is carried!

THE FLIGHT INTO EGYPT.

The huntsman is out in keen search of his prey,
Is tracking thee home; 'tis unsafe to delay—
Flee, Mother, and hide thy poor Infant awhile—
The tall reeds and rushes still bend o'er the Nile.
The fugitives flit o'er the fields bathed in light,
Down the gorge of the mountains they pass out of sight,
Escaping the vineyards and valley, they gain
Ere morning the lone desert's smooth trackless plain—
        Far and wide
        On every side
Lies the desert's yellow ocean—
        As they go,
        Cries of woe
Fill their hearts with sad emotion.

Away from the arms of his mother is torn
Each innocent image of Mary's New-born—
The shrieks of the slaughtered, and cries of despair
Are borne to the desert in each breath of air—
Hush ! infants, or Mary's poor heart will soon break,
Her own must be saved, else she would not forsake
The victims of Rama, where Rachel opprest
Bewails the foul murder of babes at the breast—
   Children blest
   Be at rest,
 Life but means to die for Jesus—
   In one breath
   Life and death
Give you all we want to ease us.

They suffer from hunger and thirst on their way,
The Mother and Child feel the sun's scorching ray,
He dries up the fountains and withers the grass,
Grey stones trace the torrents and brooks which they pass.
The Bedouin robbers have God for their guest—
Sometimes on a rock Mary gives Him the breast,
Gazelles and wild antelopes gathered around,
Half-tamed by her sight, and her lullaby's sound—
   Ah, the bliss
   Of each kiss,
 While she tends her Infant feeding !
   When He sleeps
   Then she weeps
 Thinking of Him torn and bleeding !

The desert hath dangers, but hath Egypt none?
Hath Pharaoh forgot that dark death of his son?
Their Guide through the desert will here be their shield
With him they are safe as in Nazareth's field. . .
When the Herod of hell triumphs over our hearts,
Mary's Flight is renewed, and our Jesus departs—
May we quickly repent! and, dear Mother, beg thee
To return, as thou didst to the green Galilee!
   One and all
   When we fall
  Drive from home our faithful Mother!
   Tear the nest—
   At the breast
 Strike the Babe, our beauteous Brother!

III.

THE THREE DAYS' LOSS.

How many a heart must have melted with pity,
To see the white lambs driven through Sion's city,
　　Decked out for the blood-shedding knife—
The Temple courts rang with their innocent bleating,
As though the young things were thus meekly entreating
　　For one more short summer of life—

Those feasts of the Pasch brought forebodings to Mary,
The sad mother worshipped then timid and wary,
　　And moved by those poor plaintive cries;
For, year after year, she went faithfully thither,
The true Pascal Lamb, the Divine Victim with her,
　　Her life and the light of her eyes.

Peace came, when at even the companies started
For home, and though Mary and Joseph were parted,
    The journey was one of sweet joy—
The Child, who from one to the other went straying,
Knew well how to comfort His Mother pourtraying
    The death of her beautiful Boy.

How dreadful that Pasch! when, the day's journey ended,
Woe blacker than night on the Mother descended—
    She saw that her Jesus was gone!
Men know when a sorrow will bear kind words spoken,
And none dared reply to a grief so heart-broken,
    For none could say where was her Son.

He was gone, He was gone! And darkness was falling—
He was lost, He was lost!—and silence appalling
    Brought back each unanswered lone cry—
The birds in the gloaming were greeting each other,
Then came the night's hush on the desolate Mother
    Awaiting her lost One's reply!

"Oh what have I done, that my Child should thus leave me?
Return, O my Jesus! In what did I grieve Thee?
    Art Thou gone without warning or word?
Oh! perhaps even now my Lamb bleeds on that Altar"—
The mute Angels heard her in agony falter,
    And wept at this stroke of the Sword.

Less welcome was light when it dawned on creation,
Than when the day broke on her dark desolation,
    And timidly crept up the sky—
At the first ray, with Joseph the poor Mother started.
They sped with the swiftness of love broken-hearted,
    And scanned each fresh group that drew nigh.

They asked, though she feared that her questions were bootless,
They searched, though she felt that the search would be fruitless,
    They traversed the streets and the squares—
The city was calm, so He had not been taken—
Her Child was uninjured, but she was forsaken—
    And God did not answer her prayers.

But listen! The daughters of Sion are speaking;
"Oh, whom is the fairest of women thus seeking?
    'Tis Jesus of Nazareth she seeks—
The Child whose sweet beauty attracts all beholders—
The Child with gold hair falling down on His shoulders,
    Like roses of spring are His cheeks.

"Oh fear not, sweet Lady, what harm can befall Him?
We will seek Him with thee! we will cease not to call Him—
    He soon will come back to thy arms!"
The day waned away, and the Child was still straying—
The night came again—Alas! where was He staying?
    Another long night of alarms!

Ah! worse than the pang of Saint Simeon's prediction,
Most fearfully like the foretold Crucifixion—
    Three days she confronted the Cross—
Who knows how she lived through those nights of affliction,
Ordained to foreshadow her dread dereliction
    When parted by Death not by Loss?

Ah! this is a sorrow as vast as the ocean—
Her woe is revealed in her words of emotion,
    Her language of gentle complaint.
And yet her sad question seems almost unheeded—
The work of His Father by Jesus is pleaded
    In terms of mysterious constraint.

O souls! without Jesus, and yet without sorrow,
Who put off so coldly your search till the morrow,
    Perchance till the day of your death—
Who dwell in your darkness, yet see the Truth shining,
Who harden your hearts which God's grace is inclining,
    Nor harken to what His voice saith—

Your life without Jesus is wasted and aimless—
His Mother, who lost Him yet losing was blameless,
    Now calls you from sin and from sleep.
O Mary! who sorrowing sought Him and found Him,
Lead all unto Christ, where His Flock lies around Him,
    The Shepherd who sought the lost sheep.

IV.

MEETING JESUS WITH THE CROSS.

O YE, who dwell in this great toiling town,
   Ye think your lot unknown!
   Your labour borne alone!
Through din of day, and through the gloomy night,
   And whether fall or fight,
   Your life is kept in sight—
Turn, only turn! One walks ye then must meet—
   He follows in the street—
   With Wounds in Hands and Feet!

Ye busy slaves! ye Mammon-serving men
        Of haste and silence—when
        Ye pass Him, look again!
And ye, who stand irresolute outside
        Where Shame and Sin abide—
        He passes—do not hide!
Ye homeless ones—unnamed, long gone astray—
        E'en where ye wander, pray!
        Perchance He comes that way.

Ye Poor! He sees you thrust back with your wants,
        And cruel unjust taunts,
        To Famine's fever haunts!
Ye little ones! run to Him if ye will!
        Ah! treat no children ill;
        He watches children still.
All ye! who bear grief's aching weary loads
        Along the city's roads,
        Are watched to your abodes!

By country paths, there used to stand the Cross
        'Mid primroses and moss,
        Now England mourns its loss—
From this blest sign the foolish nation fled,
        Scarce placing it with dread
        Above the sleeping dead—
Yet Faith beholds it still—In every town,
        Though men pass idly by—
        Christ comes with Cross and crown.

For this huge world of sickness, woe, and pain,
        No mortal can explain
        Without the Cross judged vain—
It is as if—e'en they can read that run—
        In those whom worldlings shun
        The Mother meets her Son—
That scene is here renewed—that mournful day,
        The Meeting on the Way—
        The silent brief delay.

Slow, slow He crept—at last He drew in sight—
    All dimmed His beauty bright—
    Extinguished all His light—
How mournfully from hair and blood He strove
    To free His eyes, and prove
    Unchanged His tender love!
But He was thrust away, and from her thrown,
    No ruth, no pity shown—
    He sank with gentle moan.

No pity shown! before His Mother's eyes—
    Regardless of her sighs,
    With oaths they made him rise!
On, ever on! spurned, beaten if He flagged
    With lash, or staves all-jagged—
    Thus was our Saviour dragged!
Will none have pity on the Mother's woe?
    None share what bends Him low,
    And save his God a blow?

How oft the works of mercy loudly cry
    For some slight sympathy,
    And we pass coldly by!
Faith warns us, but we turn away our eyes,
    While Mary sadly sighs,
    And Jesus meekly dies.
And thus we err—reluctant to relieve,
    Thus fail we to perceive
    The Sacred Hearts we grieve!

Ye rich! have pity on the toiling town!
    O hear that gentle moan!
    O see that Falling One!
And promise Mary, you will henceforth share
    The crosses mortals bear,
    As if her sons they were!
And "in the least of these His Brethren" meet
    Your Lord in every street
    With Wounds in Hands and Feet!

V.

THE CRUCIFIXION.

MAKE peace with Him ye pierced, and mourn
　　Before the day of doom—
Appease her who stood there forlorn,
　　When heaven was hid in gloom—
Ah! let us grieve we made Him die,
And caused His Mother's misery.

She shares it all, from first to last.
　　She sees and feels the worst—
She watches nails hold firm and fast
　　The Child her sweet arms nurs'd—
The little Hands that clasped her neck
Hang bleeding there, a fearful wreck!

She hears the dripping of His Blood,
    The nerves rend with the strain—
Upon the rugged, stubborn wood
    His joints are racked with pain—
He thirsts—she cannot cool His tongue—
Think, how the Mother's breast is wrung!

They stripped Him, that she may behold
    The Scourged One's beauty marred,
And call to mind the days of old,
    The manger deemed so hard—
Oh! wounded Flesh and tortured Head
Now find the Cross a harder bed!

And she, who heard the Angels sing
    Around the midnight cave,
Sees Israel crucify their King,
    And hears His people rave,
The Gentile soldiers throw the dice,
The Priests deride His sacrifice!

THE CRUCIFIXION.

She sees the heavy, thorn-wove crown
    The King of kings must wear,
His languid, tortured Head bent down
    With pain He scarce can bear,
The brutal jest, the sport uncouth,
That holds the gall unto His Mouth!

She knows the awful, life-long length
    Of those three hours to Him,
She feels the failing of His strength,
    She knows His Eyes grow dim—
And, wounded as with seven swords,
She listens to The Seven Words—

And thus she sees Him slowly sip
    The chalice He had feared,
Drain every drop with eager lip—
    His Father's Will revered
On Calvary is gladly done,
For Mary's love consoles her Son.

He falters whilst He bids farewell,
 He dares not call her Mother—
His dying last words briefly tell
 He leaves her to another—
But oh! the parting looks declare
An endless love that none may share!

She stands whilst He gives up the ghost—
 Towards her He bows His Head—
The life she gave Him He has lost,
 At last her Child is Dead—
Hers were His first and latest breath,
In Bethlem's Birth, in Calvary's Death.

We shall not, Mother! be content,
 Unless we bear His Cross,
And bravely tread the path He went,
 Unless life seems a loss,
And death a gain, our greatest gain—
To die with Christ with Him to reign!

VI.

THE TAKING DOWN FROM THE CROSS.

It is finished—It is finished—
  Still the Mother lingers there,
One by one the crowds diminished
  To their troubled homes repair,
But the faithful Mother stands,
Fastened like His Feet and Hands—

Is it then a brave thanksgiving
  Which is struggling from her heart?
Yes—that she is left here living,
  Left to bear the ache and smart—
Thanks that He will never know
The anguish of this matchless woe—

Thanks that His sweet life is taken,
    That for Him all pain is o'er,
Thanks that she remains forsaken—
    Better this, than any more
Of those plaintive moans and sighs,
Of those meek, imploring Eyes!

Thanks, brave thanks, although another
    Closes down His gentle Eyes,
Death usurping from the Mother
    Rights which all poor mothers prize,
Doing those last acts of love,
While she may not stir or move!

Cruel Death! thus darkly tracing
    On His Breast each fearful gash,
Showing her those interlacing
    Tokens of the scourge and lash—
Lift at least that tangled Hair,
Dry the crimson Blood-drops there!

THE TAKING DOWN FROM THE CROSS.

Mother, gaze! Thy Child is sleeping—
   See! in peace He takes His rest—
Mother, gaze! It soothes thy weeping,
   Calms thy bleeding, aching breast—
To that sad and mournful home
Soon its lifeless Love shall come—

On His Face, His Face—keep gazing!
   There—whatever may betide! . . .
But—she sees Longinus raising
   Lance to pierce His lifeless Side,
And gives thanks, e'en then! that she
Feels for Both the agony . . .

She may have Him now to bury—
   But, it must be quickly done:
As an Outcast, in a hurry,
   Unlamented, and alone—
Thus the Lamb who has been slain
Lies within her arms again!

See the Queen of Mercy pleading!
  Who hath mercy to bestow?
See the God of Mercy bleeding!
  Who will help to staunch the flow?
Shroud Him, He is stripped and dead—
Bear Him to His cold, hard bed.

Thanks, still thanks, that all is over,
  As she counts the countless tears
In the seamless garb our Lover
  On this day of wedding wears,
Woven in her virgin womb,
Who must hide it in the tomb!

Out upon that cold, bleak mountain
  Gleams the linen Winding-sheet,
Guiding all unto the Fountain
  Where the sad and sinful meet.
Bathe ye! in the saving Tide
Of the Saviour's riven Side! . . .

Learn to watch with resignation
  For your dear one's last faint breath!
Like true Christians, keep your station—
  Love can prove more strong than death!
Love must triumph over grief,
God be thanked for their relief.

Learn from Mary how to smother
  All wild words about your loss—
Pity that lone, helpless Mother
  Underneath the empty Cross—
And believe that she in turn
Comes to mourn with those who mourn.

Bring, then, linen to Christ's Mother,
  Sympathy from pure, clean hearts!
And, when summoned to another
  World, that hath no griefs or smarts—
As " White Linen, pure and fine,"
To adorn her will ye shine!

VII.

THE BURIAL OF JESUS.

Silence, kneel down—they come, they come—
They bear His Body to the Tomb;
   Oh, how Divine It is!
His arms stretch wide, and will not move—
That gesture of eternal love
   No one can change—'Tis His!

Foxes have holes, the birds their nest—
And now He gains a place of rest,
   Sorrowing love's last gift—
A place where He may lay His Head,
Into His borrowed, rock-hewn bed
   Jesus the mourners lift.

Holding Him clasped in sad embrace,
Farewell kiss on the tranquil Face
   Mary at length bestows—
Pale stars give light, and flowers shed
Scents round the Altar of the Dead,
   Dirge-like the night wind blows.

"Guard my Beloved—thou happy Tomb,
Chosen like me to be His home—
   Would that I too might stay!
Faithfully hide Him from men's hate—
Pity my woe—the Desolate,
   Driven so soon away!

"Father! once more He will complain!
May not His Mother still remain,
   Sadly to watch and weep?
Hindered by heartless sentinel—
Jesus! I may not stay! Farewell!
   Sleep! wearied Saviour, sleep!"

Waiting the Mother stands the Cross,
Triumphing rudely o'er her loss,
   Greeted by her sad kiss—
Waiting her lies the ransomed earth,
Helpless as infant after birth—
   She has been left for this.

Wanted by us, she stays to give
Motherly cares, and make us live.
   This is her sacrifice—
Giving up Jesus, taking John,
Creature for God, a servant for Son—
   Oh! it is dying twice!

Homeward she makes her mournful way,
Home! nay, home would have been to stay—
   Treasureless, plundered heart!
Soldiers have stolen thy Living Bread,
Will not e'en let thee mourn thy Dead,
   Forcing thee to depart. . . .

THE BURIAL OF JESUS.

Sinners! who caused His Blood to flow,
Sinners! who caused your Mother's woe,
  See her poor, outstretched hands!
Ready to play this weary part,
Ready to take you to her heart—
  Waiting for you she stands!

Must she then quit the Sacred Tomb?
Seeking her children, must she come
  Into the dark, bleak night?
Can we not spare her this last pain,
Hasten to her, with her remain—
  Win her the mourner's right?

Mary! to sin we gladly die,
In mystic death with Christ to lie
  Buried, with Him to rise—
Thy sorrows have not been in vain,
Turn on the children of thy pain,
  Mother! those gentle eyes.

OUR BLESSED LADY'S COMMUNION ON HOLY THURSDAY.

Now the Pascal lamb is eaten,
   Every legal rite is done,
And the Face of Jesus flushes,
   Loving to the end His own—
He prepares the promised Food
Of His Body and His Blood.

In another room His Mother,
   Softly weeping, prays apart,
Prays for Judas, guilty traitor,
   Prays for John upon His Heart—
Sadly does the Mother sigh,
Knowing that her Son must die.

'Twas for this His name of Jesus
  To her dearest Babe she gave—
Still she keeps the Prophet's warning
  In her heart so calm and brave,
Aching with its wound and pain,
Made to bleed yet not complain.

Gabriel is not sent with Ave
  To console so deep a grief;
But the loving Heart of Jesus
  Leaves her not without relief—
John—the loved one—at a word,
Stands the Deacon of His Lord.

Rise and eat, O Queen of sorrow!
  Lest thy strength to-morrow fail—
Thou must share and witness torments
  That will make the bravest quail—
Thus thy Son, the Royal Priest,
Bids thee to His Mystic Feast.

Once like dew-drop He descended,
  His abode in thee to take—
Now, He comes from lowly Altar
  Like the white snow's purest flake—
Gabriel calmed thy humble fears,
John is sent to stay thy tears.

Jesus seeks His place of safety
  Where His Heart first slept in rest,
For the whole world turns against Him,
  And the lance shall pierce His Breast.
Here at least—ah! let Him be,
In His own home, safe with thee!

See! the kneeling Mother gathers
  To her heart the Living Bread!
And, the Lamb of God thus given,
  John retires with reverent tread—
In her bosom once again
Is the Babe of Bethlehem lain!

OUR BLESSED LADY'S COMMUNION.

Mother! in thy prayer of rapture,
    Breathe a lowly suppliant's name—
Tell Him how my heart is burning,
    Half with love and half with shame—
Sighing, longing for its Lord,
Hungering for this Bread adored.

O may I thus shelter Jesus
    Who to me is likewise come!
And should other hearts refuse Him,
    May this ever be His home!
Make me more than ever thine,
Mary! that He may be mine.

March 25th, 1869.

AVE MARIA.

Hail Mary! through the Sacred Heart
Of Him whose Mother sweet thou art—
  Foreknown and set aside,
The Father's Daughter to be named,
The Mother of the Son proclaimed,
  The Holy Spirit's Bride.

The Blessed Trinity preferred
Thee unto others in the Word
  With everlasting choice;
And God decreed thee Advocate
Of mortals in their fallen state,
  So sweet would be thy voice.

The angels were vouchsafed the sight
Of thee and Jesus in the light
   Which burst forth at God's word—
Proud Satan and his bands were lost,
But Michael knew that Heaven's host
   Through thee would be restored.

The ancient Fathers knew before,
And pondered, in the days of yore,
   The promise of thy birth—
The thought of thee was like a stay
To prop them on their weary way
   Across an unblessed earth.

The nations all expected thee,
They longed for One to set them free,
   And knew He was thy Son—
The Prophets sang their Virgin Queen,
The Sybils too had dimly seen
   And hailed God's favoured One.

The noblest ancestry is thine,
The Patriarch, Royal, Priestly line
　In thee sublimely end.
When Joachim and Anna prayed,
Nor hoped for gift so long delayed,
　His angel God did send.

He bade them be no longer sad;
Like Sarah, Anna was made glad
　With thee, her wondrous child—
She bore a child conceived in grace,
Saved from the ruin of our race,
　Preserved all-undefiled.

Thy birth increased their mystic joy;
For Anna's bliss had no alloy
　Of fear or anxious pain—
Thy name was brought down from above,
That name of Mary Christians love,
　And none invoke in vain.

By God endowed with beauty rare,
With gifts of mind beyond compare,
  Thou wert beloved of all.
Thy parents holily restored
Their little one unto the Lord,
  In answer to His call.

Within the Temple thou didst dwell,
Child-Angel in thy sacred cell,
  Absorbed in love and prayer—
So lovely in thy innocence,
So clear in thy intelligence—
  The Marvel of all there.

The First to make the virgin's vow,
Its glory shone upon thy brow,
  In rays of heavenly light.
Thy purity made others long
For holiness which knows not wrong,
  Sin fled before thy sight.

In chanting prophecy and psalm,
In contemplation's blissful calm,
   For three things thou hast prayed—
To do God's blessed will on earth,
Her's, who would give Messias birth,
   And be her lowliest maid.

According to God's providence,
The Just man Joseph's innocence
   And virgin-marriage tie
Gave thee the shelter of his name
At Nazareth, when Gabriel came
   Upon God's embassy.

He told the Father's high behest,
He brought the Son's divine request,
   Announced the Dove's descent—
"Behold the handmaid of the Lord,
Be all according to thy word,"
   Was thy devout consent.

In thee, the virgin Paradise,
The heavenly Adam did arise,
   The Woman's Promised Seed—
The Word took flesh within thy womb,
Our nature there did God assume,
   As was of old decreed.

Enthroned within thy bosom chaste,
Thy Babe was borne with reverent haste
   Unto Judea's hills—
The Spirit filled Elizabeth,
She blessed the greatness of thy faith,
   Moved by her infant's thrills.

In Sion thou didst never raise
A psalm of David, hymn of praise,
   So sweet as thine own song—
And yet, thy silence was more sweet,—
When awed Saint Joseph would retreat,
   But feared to do thee wrong.

How blissfully the nine months sped!
What joy in gesture, look, and tread,
   In this ecstatic life!
Till with his tribe thy spouse was told
To be at Bethlehem enrolled,
   With thee his maiden-wife.

Within the inn there was no room,
So, in a wayside stable's gloom,
   In cold neglect and scorn—
The only shelter o'er thy head
A hut where cattle housed and fed—
   Thy Infant God was born.

Alas! to Bethlehem's disgrace,
A manger was the only place
   To lay thy little Dove!
Ah! Mary, thou didst first adore,
And then in ravishment outpour
   A joyful mother's love.

Around Him thou didst gently fold
The swaddling clothes, with love grown bold,
   And hush His plaining cries ;
When thou didst to thy bosom press
Thy Babe's sweet lips with fond caress,
   The Cave was Paradise.

The Shepherds hasten'd from their flocks,
And found between the ass and ox
   The new-born Saviour laid.
Rejoicingly did they depart,
But thou didst keep within thy heart
   The wonders that they said.

Thy pitying tears flowed unrestrained,
To see thy tender Infant pained
   By circumcision rites.
Next came the star-led Eastern Kings,
Who, making mystic offerings,
   Adored the Light of Lights.

There thou for forty days didst stay,
Concealed in order to obey
   A law not made for thee.
Then thou didst to the Temple take
The Lord, for holy Simeon's sake,
   Who pined to be set free.

He holds within his trembling arms
Thy Little One, whose beauty warms
   The holy old man's heart.
His happiness is not for long,
Sad prophecy succeeds his song,
   He speaks of sorrow's smart.

In silence thou didst hear his word
And make thine offering to the Lord,
   All things were rightly done—
The fledglings of a dove for thee,
The legal price to set Him free—
   Again He was thine own.

Saint Joseph in the dead of night
Was warned by angels to take flight,
   In Egypt to abide.
The trackless desert hid your way,
And baulk'd the tyrant of his prey,
   Though Rachel mourned and sigh'd.

In exile seven years go by,
When those who sought the Child's life die
   The angel speaks again—
Saint Joseph brings the Child and thee
To Nazareth in Galilee—
   There safely ye remain.

Hail Mary! plunged in sorrow's sea,
When Jesus left you secretly
   By blameless stratagem—
How wert thou with Saint Joseph pained!
Not knowing that the Child remained
   Within Jerusalem.

Upon the third day He was found
With wondering doctors all around,
   Amazed at His replies—
When thou didst use a parent's right
To question why He left your sight,
   His words caused fresh surprise.

He said: "Why did ye seek Me out,
And knew not I must be about
   My Father's business?"—Still
He went with you to Nazareth—
And, dwelling there till Joseph's death,
   Was subject to your will.

Again, at Cana, when He broke
Those years of silence, words were spoke
   In public unto thee,
Which seemed to warn thee not to press
Thy Mother-rights, though none the less
   Obedient was He.

Thy watchful eye had seen the need—
Thy gentle heart was quick to read
   The trouble, and the fear
Of those who bade ye to their feast,
When all their stock of wine decreased,
   And shame seemed drawing near.

When thou didst plead, "They have no wine!"
He seemed abruptly to decline
   To grant thy kind request—
Yet worked His first great miracle,
And changed the water from the well
   To wine, at thy behest.

Thou, too, didst journey to and fro,
And hear His words of wisdom flow
   To teach the multitude—
His virtues thou didst imitate,
And wert His meek associate
   In all His doing good.

He brought the Magdalen to thee,
And from thy honoured company
  She was not bid depart.
She found a shelter in thy name,
And honour in the place of shame,
  A new home in thy heart.

E'en when thine own sweet name was heard
Applied to others !—Still, no word
  Of thine expressed dissent.
He called His Mother everyone
By whom His Father's will was done—
  Thou, Mother, wert content !

Hail Mary ! most compassionate,
When men repaid with scorn and hate
  The goodness of thy Son—
Their persecution, envy, spite,
Made Him withdraw in unseen flight,
  Rejected by His own.

At last drew nigh the woful hour,
When Jesus used no more such power,
   But left their malice free.
He bent to John in Jordan's flood—
But, ere His Baptism of Blood,
   He came and knelt to thee.

Thou didst not grieve with sad lament
That tender Son, but didst consent—
   'Twas but the *Fiat* twice !
Yet who can tell the sea of woe
That filled thy heart to see Him go
   To make His Sacrifice ?

He, full of pity, filial grief
For thy great anguish, gave relief
   Before He would depart—
O miracle ! became thy Food—
Gave back to thee His Flesh and Blood,
   Again lived in thy heart.

With Him in spirit thou didst share
The Agony, the prostrate prayer,
　See Judas reach his prey,
Behold the traitor take thy place,
And dare to kiss the holy Face
　Which was not turned away.

Then, thou didst see the gentle Hands
Of Jesus bound in cruel bands,
　When leaving Him all fled.
Thy voiceless spirit's plaintive cry
Pursued that ruthless company
　By which thy Lamb was led.

To Annas first, to Caiphas next
They dragged Him with unjust pretext,
　And judged thy guiltless Child.
They smote His Face, His Beard they tore,
They spat—no face was e'er before
　So horribly defiled!

They left Him in that piteous plight,
And thou didst mourn throughout the night,
   Until the dreaded morn.
To Pilate then they took their prey,
Thou didst behold Him led away
   With blasphemy and scorn.

By Pilate He was sent to die
The culprit's death on Calvary—
   He passed before thine eyes.
Men saw the Son and Mother meet,
While pitying women throng'd the street,
   And rent the air with cries.

Thy Son, O weeping Mother, bent
Beneath His Cross, before thee went
   Along the mournful road;
And all the way the Victim bled
From scourgèd Flesh and tortured Head,
   Thy tears in torrents flowed.

At last He reached Mount Calvary's crown,
And gently laid His burden down—
   The Altar of His love.
He then sank down at their commands,
Held wide His gentle, weary Hands
   That love the more to prove.

The heavy hammer's sickening stroke,
The sound of flesh and iron broke
   A stillness deep as death.
Then, mangled Hands and Feet upbear
His bleeding Body in the air—
   Thou standest underneath!

All motionless thou wert below,
Erect, entranced, transfixed with woe,
   Past words, beyond belief;
Thy soul was drenched with bitterness,
Yet, ne'er did mother so express
   The majesty of grief.

He was thy Firstborn, only One,
No mother had so fair a son,
   The fruit of virgin womb;
The love which gave thy sorrow birth
Was more than any love of earth,
   No love could so consume.

Thy soul with love and sorrow burned,
Thy heart with gentlest pity yearned,
   With His thy courage tried;
In sympathy most exquisite
Thy soul unto His Soul was knit—
   Thou, too, wert crucified!

To see thee mourn was His worst grief—
To have no solace, no relief
   For anguish so intense;
By this His tender filial thought
To woe thy Harp of Joy was brought—
   Woe, like thine own, immense.

By thee the Eternal Father showed
His pity; from thy sad eyes flowed
   The tears He bade thee weep.
No angel came to comfort thee,
But in thy soul more piercingly
   The two-edged sword sank deep.

That sword the Son, thy loving Son,
In bidding thee adopt Saint John,
   Drove deeper in thy heart.
In darkest cloud the Spirit came,
And gave another dearest name
   To suit this mournful part.

Named Queen of Sorrows, second Eve,
He bade thee lift thy hands and grieve
   For all thy little ones.
Made children of The Desolate
We feel no more the hopeless fate
   Of Eva's exiled Sons.

This led thee, Mother, to contrast
Thy First and Fairest with thy last—
  His beauty, innocence,
His gentleness, His tender ways,
His youth, the sweetness of His gaze,
  His love of thee intense!

And then His Pains are thine own price,
Thy gifts are bought by sacrifice—
  For thee those Blood-drops fall.
From guilt all others are reprieved,
Immaculate thou wert conceived,
  Yet His Blood pays for all.

Thou standest here almost alone,
Save John, the Apostles all are gone—
  Thou grievest for their flight;
But still more doth thy kind heart ache
To see God's people thus forsake
  Their Glory and their Light.

Not they alone! Of all mankind
Too few are those who safety find
   In Him who dies for all.
"O earth, earth, earth, hide not My Blood,"
"Make some return of gratitude"—
   Is His appealing call.

Vile blasphemies offend His ears—
At last the poor Thief interferes,
   And makes his contrite prayer;
And thou dost see the light and grace
Illuminate that wistful face
   Instead of dark despair.

The gall is tasted—all is done—
The three Death-hours at last are gone—
   He ends His Sacrifice.
For sinful man one more loud cry—
For thee His dying Heart's last sigh—
   He bends His Head, and dies. . . .

Hail! Victim of barbarity!
Most ruthlessly compelled to see
   Thy lifeless God profaned!
Thy love was there to feel the smart,
When soldiers pierced that Sacred Heart,
   And all its Treasure drained.

Then Nicodemus sadly came
With Joseph, from the Tree of shame
   To take their Master down.
Thou didst once more thy Jesus hold—
Thy bosom knows how still and cold
   He lay there in His crown!

By Him thy broken heart was calmed,
While faltering, loving hands embalmed
   And wrapped Him in the shroud.
With haste and fear, in evening's gloom,
They left Him in the rock-hewn tomb,
   Delay was not allowed.

Forbade to stay and mourn thy loss,
Thou couldst but press upon the Cross
   Thy lips with gentle moan ;
And He was left to rest and sleep,
And thou didst go to watch and weep,
   All desolate, alone ! . . .

Hail Mary ! gladdened with the sight
Of Jesus Risen, fair and bright,
   Made happy with His voice.
How tenderly He comforts thee,
How sweetly lauds thy constancy ;
   O Queen of Heaven, rejoice !

The Forty days too swiftly sped—
To Olivet thy Jesus led
   His little flock—and there
He rose, He passed the olives tall—
With lifted Hands He blessed them all,
   And left them to thy care.

AVE MARIA.

The Holy Spirit, when He came
With parted tongues of golden flame,
   With thee found everyone.
What gifts, what messages of love
Were brought thee by the Heavenly Dove,
   From thy Ascended Son!

Hail! faithful Handmaid of the Lord,
Consenting to His parting word,
   Fulfilling His last will.
Twelve years this second Motherhood
Thy longing wistfulness withstood,
   And kept thee with us still.

O Virgin of all virgins! thou
Dost make the prayer, the ardent vow
   To aid the ministry.
If Peter preach, if Paul dispute,
Thy silent prayers procure the fruit—
   On thee they all rely.

How calm and sweet was thy content,
When Gabriel, for the last time sent,
   Brought greetings from on high—
Transported from each distant·land,
The Apostles kissed thy queenly hand,
   Allowed to see thee die.

He comes, He comes, thy Absent One—
Thy loving God, thy loving Son,
   Thy soul darts to His Breast!
He draws thee closer to His Heart—
No more the Son and Mother part—
   He bears thee to thy rest!

In light of glory, floods of bliss,
The Godhead's infinite Abyss
   Now face to face is seen;
The Father, Son, and Holy Ghost
Present thee to the angelic host,
   And crown thee Heaven's Queen.

Thy Son hath one more blissful task,
Which love and honour justly ask
  For her who gave Him birth—
He bids thy Body also rise,
And so transplants to Paradise
  The Lily of the earth.

Hail, Queen of Heaven! enthroned on high—
Thy crown befits thy dignity,
  Great Mother of our God!
Upon thy Heart the angels look,
That sinless Heart, from whence He took
  His Body and His Blood.

Yet we are not like orphans left,
Of thy sweet tenderness bereft,
  Thou art our Mother still,
Our Advocate, our Refuge, Friend,
Life, Hope, and Sweetness, who dost send
  A balm for every ill.

O Mother! who hast prayed and wept
For me, thy worthless son, accept
   This Ave—e'en from me.
I fain would hail thee with each breath,
Until the hour of my death,
   And for Eternity!

INNOCENCE AND PENANCE.

Across this wide world's sea
  Two consort ships are sailing;
I pray you list to me
  Their history unveiling.

The one is snowy white,
  And lightly she is laden;
Her sails are new, and bright
  As robe of bridal maiden.

Her sister's sails are red,
  With rents in many places,
Which tell of tempests dread,
  As seams in sad men's faces.

In company they sail
　　Through fair and stormy weather;
They ever keep in hail,
　　And ride the waves together.

Of faultless symmetry
　　They brave fierce winds unshaken;
For from the same good tree
　　The beams of both are taken.

They sail by day and night,
　　In each the deck is crowded;
In one all robes are white,
　　In black the rest are shrouded.

Across the tranquil sea,
　　Like distant church bells ringing,
Oft steals a melody
　　Of unseen angels singing;

And like a message sent,
   Where'er these ships pass sailing,
With Ocean's music blent
   Come sounds of joy and wailing.

At night a lustrous star
   Directs their gentle motion,
And silvers from afar
   Their smooth track on the ocean.

Towards the west they steer,
   And, when the sun is going,
If seen, alike appear
   In one gold sunset glowing. . . .

Thus Penance, Innocence
   Both make the voyage to Heaven;
One takes the Sinless hence,
   Her sister the Forgiven.

With Mary's joys one rings,
   From her come sounds of gladness;
Her griefs the other sings
   In words of tender sadness.

Their beams of the Saviour's Cross—
   Their Star most Holy Mary—
They meet no harm, no loss,
   And reach God's Sanctuary.

One golden light, one feast
   Await all souls in Heaven,
The greatest and the least—
   Unfallen and Forgiven.

www.ingramcontent.com/pod-product-compliance
Lightning Source LLC
Chambersburg PA
CBHW020242170426
43202CB00008B/196